Redeemed

30 Days to Healing, Wholeness & Holy Fire

ROSE METHENY

Redeemed: 30 Days to Healing, Wholeness & Holy Fire—A 30-Day Devotional

ISBN 979-8-9992180-2-5

Cover Design & Interior Layout: Brandi Lariscy-Avant

Published by: Grace and Glow Press

Scripture References:

Unless otherwise noted, all Scripture is taken from the New Living Translation (NLT) and the English Standard Version (ESV).

This devotional is a work of nonfiction and reflects the author's personal experiences, prayer life, and walk with Jesus Christ. Some names and identifying details have been changed to protect the privacy of others.

This 30-day devotional was prayerfully written to meet you in your quiet moments — with Scripture, truth, and the healing presence of God. May every page draw you deeper into the Word and closer to the One who restores.

For speaking inquiries, book clubs, or bulk orders:

www.rosemetheny.com | hello@rosemetheny.com

Dear Beautiful One,

First, I want to say this: I'm so proud of you.

The fact that you're holding this devotional means you're choosing to walk with Jesus through some of the most sacred and vulnerable places of your heart. That's not small. That's brave.

This devotional was born from one sacred morning of journaling during prayer—when I poured my heart out to Jesus, not knowing it would become the beginning of something so much bigger. That moment became *Redeemed*… and this devotional was created to walk you deeper into your own story with Him.

I know what it's like to feel broken, forgotten, ashamed. But I also know what it's like to be found, forgiven, and redeemed.

These 30 days aren't about perfection. They're about permission—to pause, to feel, to hope, to heal.

Each day, you'll find scripture, a word of encouragement, reflection questions, and prayer. But more than that, I hope you'll find yourself again… and the loving voice of a Father who never once let go.

You're not too far gone.nYou're not too broken. You're not behind. You're beloved. You're becoming. You're redeemed.

I'm walking this journey with you—hand in hand with the One who makes all things new.

With all my love,
Rose

DEDICATION

To Jesus—

My Savior, my Healer, my Redeemer. This is all for You. You lifted me
out of the pit and placed my feet on solid ground. Every page of this
devotional is an offering—born from pain, redeemed by grace, and
written through Your strength. Thank You for rescuing me, renewing
me, and showing me that nothing is wasted in Your hands. May every
word point back to You.

To Larry—

My honey, my covering, my safe place. Thank you for loving every
healing version of me. Your steady presence and unwavering support
have been God's grace in human form. I love you endlessly.

To my son Chris, and my bonus sons Zach and Spencer—

Thank you for being part of the story God is still writing in and through
my life. Chris, you've been my reason to rise, to fight, to heal, and to
become the woman God created me to be. Zach and Spencer, thank
you for welcoming me into your lives with grace and love. Each of
you has a special place in my heart. I'm so proud of the men you are.
May you always know how deeply you are loved—and may you always
know Jesus for yourselves.

To the reader—

Beautiful soul, thank you for inviting this devotional into your life. I
pray it meets you right where you are and reminds you that healing is
possible, hope is alive, and Jesus is near. Keep seeking, keep healing,
keep shining. You are seen, known, and so very loved.

ACKNOWLEDGMENTS

To Joanie and Jenni—
Thank you for your amazing support, love, and crazy skills! Your brilliance, encouragement, and creativity helped carry this project from idea to reality. I couldn't have done this without you.

To my prayer warrior sisters—
You held me up in the Spirit when I didn't even have the words. Thank you for covering me, interceding for me, and reminding me I wasn't alone in this. A special thank you to Pat, Ms. Susie, Debra, Diana and Ms. Angie—your prayers meant more than I can ever express. This devotional was birthed in prayer, and I know heaven heard every cry.

TABLE OF CONTENTS

HOW TO USE THIS DEVOTIONAL

This 30-day devotional was written for the woman who's been through some things. The one who's tried to move on but still feels stuck. The one who loves Jesus but is still healing. The one who wonders if freedom is really for her.

Each day includes a Scripture, a short devotion, a reflection prompt, and a prayer. There's no pressure to do it perfectly or on a strict timeline—this is your space to slow down, breathe, and heal with God.

And most importantly: Invite the Holy Spirit to guide you. These aren't just words to read—this is space for encounter. Let Him speak. Let Him comfort. Let Him bring up what He wants to heal.

Here's how to walk through it:

Start with the Scripture.

- Read it slowly. Let it speak to you. If it's hard to believe right now, that's okay—just sit with it.

- Read the devotional. Each one comes from real-life healing and real-life Jesus. These aren't "pretty" devotionals. They're *honest*.

- Reflect with the prompt. Let your heart answer honestly. Don't rush past what stirs. These questions are meant to draw you deeper.

- Pray the prayer. Say it out loud. Make it your own. Ask the Holy Spirit to meet you in the middle of it.

Come as you are. Cry if you need to. Laugh when joy surprises you. Let this be holy ground.

You are not alone. You are not too far gone. You are being *redeemed*.

Week One

Who I Am Now
(Identity & Redemption)

Isaiah 43:1 (NIV) *"Do not fear, for I have redeemed you; I have summoned you by name; you are mine."*

Prayer to Begin the Week:

Jesus, show me the truth of who I am in You. I release the lies I've believed about my worth. Help me see myself through Your eyes—whole, loved, and called.

Amen.

Redeemed Means Rewritten

Joel 2:25 (NIV) *"I will repay you for the years the locusts have eaten…"*

For so long, I thought "redeemed" just meant forgiven. Like God looked at my mess and said, "It's okay, I'll let it go."

But redemption? It's so much deeper than that.

God didn't just clean up my story. He *rewrote* it.

He stepped into the pages soaked in trauma, addiction, shame, and self-destruction—And with His mercy, He picked up the pen.

He didn't ignore what happened. He *transformed it.* The years I thought were wasted? He's using them to help others find healing. The pain I tried to bury? He's turning it into purpose. The things I never thought I'd speak of again? They're now chapters in a story that sets women free.

Redemption isn't just about erasing the past. It's about reclaiming it for glory. It's about turning *what broke you* into *what builds someone else.* It's God whispering, "I see it all—and I'm not done writing."

Reflection

What parts of your story have you tried to cross out or hide? What if those very places are the ones God wants to use for His glory?

Are you willing to hand Him the pen?

_____

_____

_____

_____

_____

Prayer

Jesus, thank You for not just forgiving me... but *redeeming* me. Thank You for rewriting the pages I thought were ruined. I surrender the broken chapters—the ones I'm scared to look at—and I trust You to bring beauty from them. Turn my wounds into words. My pain into purpose. I give You the pen, Lord. Write something eternal.

Amen.

Day 2

DEVOTIONAL

He Didn't Flinch

John 4:29 (NIV) *"Come, see a man who told me everything I ever did. Could this be the Messiah?"*

She didn't hide her story—she *led* with it.

The Samaritan woman didn't go back to town saying, "I met a prophet who made me feel good about myself." She said, "Come meet the One who saw it *all*—and still stayed."

That line wrecks me every time: He told me everything I ever did. And you know what? He didn't flinch.

He didn't shame her. Didn't walk away. Didn't tell her to clean herself up first.

He just loved her. Right there in her truth. Right there in her tangled history. Right there in the part of her story she probably prayed no one would ever know.

He brought it to the surface—not to humiliate her, but to *heal* her.

And sis… He's still doing that today. With you. With me. With every woman who thinks her past disqualifies her from holy encounters.

He already knows your whole story. And He's not scared of it.

He's the God who sees it all—and stays.

Reflection

What parts of your story are you still hiding because you're afraid of rejection? What if you let Jesus sit with you there? What would happen if you believed that He doesn't flinch—even at *that* part?

_____

_____

_____

_____

_____

Prayer

Jesus, thank You for seeing it all — and choosing to stay. I don't have to hide with You. You're not afraid of my story, my scars, or my struggles. Come sit with me in the places I've buried. And gently, lovingly, rewrite them with Your grace.

Amen.

The Pain Behind the Smile

Isaiah 61:3 (NLT) *"To all who mourn in Zion, He will give a crown of beauty for ashes, a joyous blessing instead of mourning, festive praise instead of despair..."*

We learn how to hide early. The practiced smile. The "I'm fine" on autopilot. The perfectly curated outside that keeps the brokenness inside untouched and unseen.

But Jesus? He sees past all that.

He sees the pain behind the smile. The ache behind the eyes. The girl holding it all together in public while falling apart in private.

And He doesn't pull away. He leans in.

Not to expose you—but to heal you. Not to shame you—but to *set you free.*

You weren't made to live in survival mode. You were made to *thrive in truth.* To trade your ashes for beauty. To swap your mourning for dancing. To take off the mask and finally breathe.

You can let go of the performance. Jesus wants the *real* you—not the polished version.

And when you bring Him the pain? He brings you healing. Not just for your smile. But for your *soul.*

Reflection

Where are you still performing instead of healing? What would it look like to bring the "hidden you" fully into the light with Jesus?

Ask yourself: What am I hiding… and why?

_____

_____

_____

_____

_____

Prayer

Jesus, You see me fully—and still call me beautiful. I don't want to hide anymore. Take the pain I've tucked behind my smile. Heal it. Redeem it. Replace it with real joy, real peace, real freedom. I trust You with the unfiltered version of me.

Amen.

Day 4

When the Silence Hurts

Psalm 34:18 (NIV) *"The Lord is close to the brokenhearted and saves those who are crushed in spirit."*

There's a silence that isn't peaceful. It's heavy. It lingers like a fog, thick with unanswered questions and unspoken pain.

You prayed. You cried. You begged. And all you got back was... *silence.*

It's one of the loneliest places to be—when your heart is shattered and Heaven feels quiet. But just because God is silent doesn't mean He's absent.

In fact, sometimes the silence is where He's *closest.*

He's near in the sobs no one else hears. Near in the stillness when you're too tired to speak. Near in the moments where you're holding on by a thread.

God doesn't need noise to move. He works in the quiet. He heals in the stillness. He listens to the ache.

The silence isn't the end of your story—it's the *space* where healing begins. Let Him meet you there.

Reflection

Have you ever felt like God was silent when you needed Him most? What would it look like to sit in the silence and trust He's still present?

Ask yourself: Am I listening for comfort… or trusting that He's already near?

_____

_____

_____

_____

_____

Prayer

God, the silence is hard. It makes me feel forgotten, unseen, alone. But I believe Your Word—that You are *close* to the brokenhearted So I choose to believe You're near, even when I can't feel You. Sit with me in the stillness. Speak to my soul, even when Heaven feels quiet. Remind me I'm never alone.

Amen.

DEVOTIONAL

Shame Off Me

Romans 8:1 (NLT) *"So now there is no condemnation for those who belong to Christ Jesus."*

Shame is loud. It echoes through your thoughts. It twists your memories. It convinces you that you'll *never* be clean. *Never* be good enough. *Never* outrun what happened.

But shame is a liar. And Jesus came to shut it down.

He doesn't just cover shame—He *removes* it. He doesn't say, "I'll forgive you, but let's not talk about that part." He says, "Let's bring it into the light—and let Me heal it for good."

Condemnation is not from God. It's the voice of the enemy trying to keep you tied to something Jesus already set you free from.

If you belong to Christ, you are not what happened to you. You are not what you did. You are not what was done in the dark.

You are clean. You are whole. You are His.

Sis, the cross didn't halfway redeem you. It *fully* did.

So today, drop the shame. Walk in grace. Say it out loud: "Shame off me—in Jesus' name."

Reflection

What's one area of your life where shame still tries to speak? Are you willing to replace that voice with truth today?

Ask yourself: Would I say to someone else what shame says to me?

_____

_____

_____

_____

_____

Prayer

Jesus, shame has held onto me for too long. I give it to You. Every lie, every memory, every weight I've carried—take it. Remind me that I am not condemned. I am covered in grace, washed in love, and forever free. Shame off me. Truth on me.

Amen.

Day 6

DEVOTIONAL

From Surviving to Living

John 10:10 (NIV) *"I have come that they may have life, and have it to the full."*

Survival mode feels normal when you've lived in pain. You learn how to fake a smile. You function through the numbness. You perform. You protect. You *endure.*

But sis—Jesus didn't die so you could *just survive.* He came so you could *live.* Fully. Freely. Boldly.

Survival mode may have helped you get through the trauma—But it's not meant to be your home.

You were created to breathe deep. To laugh loud. To rest without guilt. To *live* without fear.

That means no more apologizing for healing. No more shrinking back. No more calling the bare minimum "enough" when God called you to *overflow.*

You're not just someone who made it out. You're someone God is raising up.

You're no longer stuck. You're *alive.*

Reflection

Where in your life are you still operating in survival mode? What does "living fully" look like for you right now?

Ask yourself: Have I confused functioning with thriving?

Prayer

Jesus, I don't want to just survive anymore. I want the life You died to give me—a full, free, joy-filled life. Help me release survival mode. Teach me to receive the good things without fear. I believe I was made for more—and I say yes to it today.

Amen.

Day 7

Held in the Dark

Psalm 139:11–12 (NLT) *"I could ask the darkness to hide me and the light around me to become night—but even in darkness I cannot hide from you. To you the night shines as bright as day. Darkness and light are the same to you."*

There were seasons I wanted to disappear. To hide from the world. To hide from myself. Even to hide from God.

Because the dark felt safer than being seen.

But you know what? Even in the dark, *He was there.*

When the pain was too deep to pray When the numbness felt easier than facing it—When the night lasted longer than I thought I could stand—He never let go.

God doesn't flinch in the darkness. He steps into it with open arms and gentle light.

You might not have *felt* Him in those moments… But He was there. Holding you. Covering you. Weeping with you. And *waiting* to bring you out of it—not with shame, but with love.

You don't have to be afraid of the dark anymore. You are fully known, and still fully held.

Reflection

Where have you tried to hide—from others, from God, even from yourself?

Ask yourself: What if the very place I thought was abandoned... was where God was holding me all along?

_____

_____

_____

_____

_____

Prayer

God, thank You for being with me—even in the darkest moments. Thank You for never looking away. For never giving up on me. For holding me when I didn't know how to hold myself together. Bring light into the places I've hidden. And remind me that I've never been alone. Not for one second.

Amen.

Day 8

Unfiltered—A Journal from the Pain

2 Corinthians 12:9 (NIV) *"But He said to me, 'My grace is sufficient for you, for My power is made perfect in weakness.' Therefore I will boast all the more gladly about my weaknesses, so that Christ's power may rest on me."*

We live in a filtered world. Smoothed skin. Cropped photos. Curated captions. We post what we want others to see. And we hide the rest.

But healing doesn't happen through filters. Healing happens in truth.

There were journal entries I wrote that never saw the light of day. Ugly tears. Raw confessions. Pain I didn't even have words for. But Jesus read every page. And He *didn't turn away.*

He didn't say, "That's too much." He didn't tell me to clean it up.

He sat with me in it. And then—little by little—He began to heal it.

Sis, your pain doesn't disqualify you. Your brokenness doesn't embarrass God. In fact, it's the very place His power shines the brightest.

Let this be the season where you show up unfiltered. Messy. Honest. Open. Not for the world—but for *your healing.* And for His glory.

Reflection

Have you been afraid to sit with your own pain? Are you still trying to present the "strong version" of yourself to God?

Ask yourself: What would it look like to invite Jesus into the pages I've kept hidden?

Prayer

Jesus, I give You my unfiltered story. The messy pages. The broken thoughts. The pain I've tried to push down. I don't want to fake it with You. I want to heal with You. Thank You for loving me in every chapter. Write something beautiful with what I've handed You.

Amen.

DEVOTIONAL

I Am Not What Happened to Me

Isaiah 43:1 (NIV) *"Do not fear, for I have redeemed you; I have summoned you by name; you are mine."*

You are not what happened to you. You are not your trauma. You are not the mistakes. You are not the decisions made *for* you without your consent. You are not the abuse. You are not the labels. You are not the seasons where it felt like everything fell apart.

You are *His.* Redeemed. Restored. Named. Chosen.

The enemy loves to attach your identity to your pain—but Jesus attaches it to your *redemption.*

When you walk in healing, it's not about forgetting what happened— it's about refusing to let it define you anymore.

Yes, your story shaped you. But it doesn't get the final word. God does.

You are not what happened. You are *what Jesus did about it.*

Reflection

Where have you unknowingly tied your identity to your past pain?

Ask yourself: What labels have I carried that God never gave me?

_____

_____

_____

_____

_____

Prayer

Jesus, thank You for reminding me who I am—and *whose* I am. I break every false label, every identity rooted in pain. You call me daughter. You call me chosen. You call me redeemed. Help me walk in that truth today—fully, freely, boldly.

Amen.

Week Two

Forgiveness, Trust & Letting Go

Psalm 55:22 (NIV) *"Cast your cares on the Lord and He will sustain you; He will never let the righteous be shaken."*

Prayer to Begin the Week:

Jesus, I give You what I've been holding. The pain, the blame, the fear. I trust You with it all. Help me loosen my grip so You can heal what I've tried to manage alone.

Amen.

DEVOTIONAL

Forgiving What Still Hurts

Matthew 18:21–22 (NIV) *"Then Peter came to Jesus and asked, 'Lord, how many times shall I forgive my brother or sister who sins against me? Up to seven times?' Jesus answered, 'I tell you, not seven times, but seventy-seven times.'"*

Forgiveness isn't a one-time thing. Especially when the pain lingers.

There were people who hurt me so deeply, I didn't even realize how tightly I was holding on to it. The memories would flash without warning. The sting would resurface. And I'd wonder… "Haven't I already forgiven them?"

But forgiveness isn't just a feeling—it's a *decision*. Sometimes one we have to make again and again. And again.

You're not weak for still feeling pain. You're human. You're healing. And healing takes *time*.

Forgiveness doesn't say, "What they did was okay." It says, "I refuse to carry this anymore."

Jesus isn't asking you to forget. He's inviting you to be free.

Sis, don't let unforgiveness keep you tethered to the thing that broke you. Release it. Even if you have to do it 77 x 7 times a day.

Reflection

Who do you still feel tension, anger, or pain around—even silently?

Ask yourself: What am I hoping to gain by holding onto this… and what might I gain if I let it go?

_____

_____

_____

_____

_____

Prayer

Lord, this still hurts. You know what they did. You saw it all. And I trust that You are just and You are kind. Help me forgive—even when the pain feels fresh. Help me release what I was never meant to carry. I don't want to be tied to this anymore. I choose freedom. I choose You.

Amen.

Day 11

I'm Not Her Anymore

2 Corinthians 5:17 (NLT) *"This means that anyone who belongs to Christ has become a new person. The old life is gone; a new life has begun!"*

Sometimes the hardest part of healing isn't letting go of *them*—it's letting go of *her*. The version of you that lived in survival. The one who accepted less. The one who numbed the pain. The one who wore the guilt and shame like a second skin. The one who kept quiet, stayed small, or settled because she thought that's all she deserved.

But you're not her anymore.

You are redeemed. You are restored. You are *reborn.*

You don't have to live like the old you—even if some people still try to hold you to it. You are not defined by your past. You are defined by what Jesus did — and what He's still doing in you now.

So give yourself permission to evolve. To heal. To rise. To take up space as the *new creation* you already are.

Look back only to praise God for how far He's brought you—Then *keep walking forward in freedom.*

Reflection

Is there a version of your past self you're still identifying with, even after healing?

Ask yourself: What would it look like to fully step into the new me God has created?

_____

_____

_____

_____

_____

Prayer

Jesus, thank You for the grace to grow. Thank You for not holding me to who I used to be. Help me release every false identity, every old mindset, every broken version of me that no longer serves who You're shaping me into. I am not her anymore—and I praise You for that.

Amen.

DEVOTIONAL

Delayed Doesn't Mean Denied

Habakkuk 2:3 (NLT) *"This vision is for a future time. It describes the end, and it will be fulfilled. If it seems slow in coming, wait patiently, for it will surely take place. It will not be delayed."*

There were moments I was sure God forgot about me. I saw others getting blessed, moving forward, walking into new seasons…And I was still stuck in the same valley. Still waiting. Still praying. Still hoping something would finally shift.

I started to wonder: Did I miss it? Did I mess it up? Was I too late… or not enough?

But then God whispered: *"Delayed doesn't mean denied."*

God doesn't forget. And He's never late. When He speaks a promise, He *will* fulfill it—even if it takes longer than you thought. The waiting isn't punishment… it's preparation.

Sometimes the delay is where character is shaped. Where roots grow deeper. Where distractions fall off so you can hear Him clearly.

If He said it—He meant it. Your breakthrough is on the way. Wait well. Believe big. Keep going.

Reflection

Where have you started to question God's timing—or even His plan?

Ask yourself: Am I trusting His character even when I don't understand His calendar?

Prayer

God, I trust You—even when it's hard. Even when the waiting feels long. Even when it seems like nothing's moving. Remind me that You're not late. You're working behind the scenes. Give me the strength to wait well—with hope, with peace, and with faith.

Amen.

Don't Look Back, You're Not There Anymore

Scripture: Philippians 3:13–14 (NIV) *"But one thing I do: Forgetting what is behind and straining toward what is ahead, I press on toward the goal to win the prize for which God has called me heavenward in Christ Jesus."*

There was a season when I couldn't stop looking back. Back at the trauma. Back at the shame. Back at what I should've done differently. Back at who I used to be.

It was like dragging around the ghost of my past—and wondering why I couldn't walk in freedom.

But the truth is: You can't move forward if you're staring in the rearview mirror.

You're not her anymore. You've been healed. You've been changed. You've been *redeemed.*

There is nothing left for you in that old place. No healing in reliving the guilt. No breakthrough in reopening wounds.

Jesus already did the work. Now it's time to let go, look forward, and *walk in newness.*

You are not where you came from. You are where God is leading you.

Reflection

Is there a memory, mistake, or moment you keep replaying—even though it no longer defines you?

Ask yourself: What am I afraid to release… and what would it feel like to finally let it go?

_____

_____

_____

_____

_____

Prayer

Jesus, thank You for pulling me out of my past. I don't want to live in what was. I want to walk in what *is*. Help me release the moments I've held onto too tightly. Help me fix my eyes on You—the Author and Finisher of my story. Today, I press forward.

Amen.

Day 14

Peace Is a Miracle Too

Scripture: John 14:27 (NIV) *"Peace I leave with you; my peace I give you. I do not give to you as the world gives. Do not let your hearts be troubled and do not be afraid."*

Sometimes we think miracles have to be loud. Obvious. Dramatic. Fire-from-Heaven type moments. But sis, let me tell you…

Waking up and not feeling anxious? That's a miracle. Going a whole day without replaying the trauma? Miracle. Being able to rest. Laugh. Breathe deeply. Peace? That's a *holy* miracle.

Because when you've lived through chaos, when your nervous system has been wired for survival, when you've fought to feel "normal" again…

Peace feels like a radical, God-breathed gift.

It's not always loud. Sometimes it's just the absence of the ache. The quiet of a soul no longer at war with itself. The steady presence of Jesus, holding you still inside when everything else used to spin.

Don't discount what God has done just because it feels gentle. Peace is powerful. And it's *proof* that healing is happening.

Reflection

Have you overlooked the quiet ways God has been healing you?

Ask yourself: What does peace look like for me now—and how has God already answered that prayer?

_____

_____

_____

_____

_____

Prayer

Jesus, thank You for peace. Not the kind that the world gives—but the kind that comes from You. Calm my anxious heart. Show me how far You've brought me. Help me celebrate the stillness, the slowness, the steady ground beneath my feet. I don't take peace for granted. I know it's a miracle.

Amen.

Week Three

Becoming—
Softness, Strength & Growth

Scripture: Philippians 1:6 (NIV) *"…He who began a good work in you will carry it on to completion until the day of Christ Jesus."*

Prayer to Begin the Week:

God, thank You for being patient with me. Thank You for growing me gently, even when I can't see it. I surrender the pressure to perform. Keep shaping me—I trust Your hands.

Amen.

Day 14

Breathing Again

Scripture: Genesis 2:7 (NLT) *"Then the Lord God formed the man from the dust of the ground. He breathed the breath of life into the man's nostrils, and the man became a living person."*

There was a time I didn't realize I had stopped breathing. Not physically… but spiritually. Emotionally. Deep in my soul.

I was surviving. Functioning. Going through the motions. But joy? Rest? Ease?

Gone.

Trauma will do that. So will shame. So will years of pretending you're okay when you're breaking inside.

But then—slowly, gently—God began to breathe life into me again. Not with pressure. Not with performance. Just presence.

He reminded me that I wasn't created to stay in survival mode. I was created to *live*. To *breathe*. To *thrive* in His love.

Sis, if you've been holding your breath for too long, it's okay to exhale. God is breathing into you again. Let yourself live.

Reflection

Where have you been holding your breath in life—afraid to feel, afraid to rest, afraid to hope?

Ask yourself: What would it look like to let God breathe into that space again?

Prayer

God, sometimes I forget how to just *be*. I've held my breath for so long, afraid to fall apart, afraid to hope again. But You are the breath in my lungs. You are the calm in my chest. So today, I exhale. And I invite You to breathe into me again—softly, sweetly, fully.

Amen.

Day 15

This Didn't Ruin You

Romans 8:28 (NIV) *"And we know that in all things God works for the good of those who love him, who have been called according to his purpose."*

There was a time I thought, "This is it. This is the thing that's going to break me." The trauma. The betrayal. The moment everything came crashing down.

I didn't know how I'd get up. How I'd keep going. How I'd ever feel whole again.

But I did. Because God was already standing in the wreckage—holding redemption in His hands.

He didn't cause the pain. But He refused to waste it.

Every moment of heartbreak? He's using it to build strength. Every lie you believed? He's rewriting it with truth. Every tear? He's counting it—and trading it for purpose.

You made it. Maybe limping. Maybe messy. But *you're still here.*

This didn't ruin you. It revealed you. It refined you. It rooted you deeper in Jesus than you've ever been before. You are not ruined. You are *redeemed.*

Reflection

What part of your story still feels like a "ruin"—something broken beyond repair?

Ask yourself: What if this isn't where it ends, but where something beautiful begins?

_____

_____

_____

_____

_____

Prayer

Jesus, thank You that nothing in my life is wasted. Even the hardest moments—You hold them with care and turn them into something I couldn't imagine. Remind me that I am not ruined. I am not too far gone. You are still writing my story—and it ends in redemption.

Amen.

Day 16

DEVOTIONAL

You Don't Have to Earn This

Ephesians 2:8–9 (NIV) *"For it is by grace you have been saved, through faith—and this is not from yourselves, it is the gift of God—not by works, so that no one can boast."*

When you've been through trauma, performance becomes survival. Be strong. Be good. Be quiet. Be helpful. Be *enough.*

So when healing comes, it can feel… hard to receive. Like you have to work for it. Earn it. Deserve it.

But grace? Grace doesn't work like that.

God isn't healing you because you did all the right things. He's healing you because *He loves you.* He's restoring you because *you're His.* Not because you prayed perfectly, or journaled enough, or forgave fast enough.

Healing is *not* a reward. It's a gift. And you are allowed to receive it without guilt, shame, or striving.

Jesus already paid for it. You don't have to hustle for what He bled to give.

So breathe, sis. Let it in. Let Him love you back to life.

Reflection

Where are you still striving, performing, or trying to "earn" what God already gave you?

Ask yourself: What would change if I truly received His grace like a gift—instead of a goal?

Prayer

Jesus, I lay down the pressure to perform. I've carried this weight for too long. Help me receive Your grace—not just in my mind, but deep in my spirit. Remind me that I don't have to earn what You've already given. I am loved. I am chosen. I am enough—because You are.

Amen.

Day 17

DEVOTIONAL

You're Allowed to Speak

Proverbs 31:26 (NIV) *"She speaks with wisdom, and faithful instruction is on her tongue."*

For so long, I didn't speak up. Not about the pain. Not about the fear. Not about the boundaries that were crossed or the wounds that never healed.

I stayed quiet. Because somewhere along the line, I was taught that silence was strength. That being "the bigger person" meant shrinking down. That my voice was *too much, too loud, too messy.*

But God never asked me to disappear.

In fact, He gave me a voice *on purpose.*

Your story? It matters. Your perspective? It carries weight. Your truth? It's powerful—and someone *needs* to hear it.

You are not just allowed to speak—you are *called* to.

And when your voice is rooted in healing and love, it becomes a weapon against shame, injustice, and fear.

So no more shrinking. No more second-guessing. You're allowed to speak. *And Heaven backs your voice.*

Reflection

Where have you silenced yourself out of fear, shame, or people-pleasing?

Ask yourself: What truth have I been afraid to say out loud—even just to myself?

_____

_____

_____

_____

_____

Prayer

God, thank You for giving me a voice. For reminding me that my truth matters. I lay down fear, shame, and all the lies that told me to stay quiet. Teach me to speak with boldness and grace. To share from a healed place. To tell my story, because it carries freedom for someone else. I am no longer silent.

Amen.

You're Not Hard to Love

Zephaniah 3:17 (NIV) *"The Lord your God is with you, the Mighty Warrior who saves. He will take great delight in you; in his love He will no longer rebuke you, but will rejoice over you with singing."*

There were seasons I believed I was too much. Too emotional. Too messy. Too broken. Too complicated. Too scarred.

And other seasons where I believed I wasn't enough. Not good enough. Not pretty enough. Not strong enough. Not pure enough.

Somewhere in between, I made peace with the lie: "I must be hard to love."

But that was *never* God's voice.

Because He doesn't love me based on my performance. He doesn't flinch at my wounds or measure my worth against perfection.

He delights in me. He sings over me. He calls me *His beloved.*

I am not hard to love. I am wildly, relentlessly, unconditionally loved.

And so are you.

If you've been carrying that lie—it's time to lay it down. Let the truth of Heaven rewrite the story in your heart.

You are not hard to love. You are already *so deeply loved.*

Reflection

What lie have you believed about your worth or lovability?

Ask yourself: If I believed I was easy to love… how would I speak to myself differently?

Prayer

God, thank You for loving me without conditions. Thank You for seeing past my past—and loving the real me. I release the lie that I am hard to love. I let go of every word, wound, and voice that told me otherwise. Help me receive Your love fully… and live like it's true.

Amen.

Day 19

DEVOTIONAL

The Part I Still Don't Understand

Proverbs 3:5–6 (NIV) *"Trust in the Lord with all your heart and lean not on your own understanding; in all your ways submit to Him, and He will make your paths straight."*

There's a part of my story I still don't understand. A moment that didn't get a bow tied around it. A wound that didn't come with an explanation. A pain I carried that still hasn't made sense—even after the healing.

I've asked God, "Why?" more times than I can count. Why did that happen? Why didn't You stop it? Why did I have to walk through that when others didn't?

And you know what? He hasn't always answered the way I hoped. But He *has* held me through it. And slowly, gently… He's taught me that trust doesn't require full understanding.

Some things won't make sense on this side of eternity. But even when I don't get the answer—I still get *Him.*

And that's enough.

You don't have to understand it all to move forward. You just have to trust the One who does.

Reflection

What part of your story still doesn't make sense — the piece you wrestle with, question, or try to avoid?

Ask yourself: What would it look like to trust God with that part... even if I never get the full answer?

_____

_____

_____

_____

_____

Prayer

God, this part still hurts. This part still confuses me. But I trust You. Even when I don't have the "why." Even when I don't get closure. Even when I wish it played out differently. You are still good. You are still faithful. And I place this piece of my story in Your hands again today.

Amen.

Day 20

DEVOTIONAL

You're Growing Even If You Don't Feel It

Galatians 6:9 (NIV) *"Let us not become weary in doing good, for at the proper time we will reap a harvest if we do not give up."*

Not every healing moment feels like a breakthrough. Sometimes, it feels like waking up and choosing not to numb. Sometimes, it's crying your way through a prayer you don't have words for. Sometimes, it's showing up when you'd rather stay hidden.

That's growth.

But when you've spent years in survival mode, it's easy to feel like you're stuck—like you should be "further along" by now. Like you're failing because you still have bad days. But sis… growth doesn't always feel like victory. Sometimes it just feels like *faithfulness.*

Healing isn't always loud. Sometimes it's steady. Sometimes it's silent. But it's happening.

Heaven is watching. God sees it all. And He's *so proud of you.*

Don't give up. You're growing—even when you can't see it yet.

Reflection

Where have you been dismissing your own progress—or comparing your healing to someone else's?

Ask yourself: What's one quiet way I've grown that deserves to be celebrated?

_____

_____

_____

_____

_____

Prayer

God, thank You for the slow miracles. For the growth I don't always feel but that You're working in me anyway. Help me stop measuring myself by the world's standards—or my own expectations. Help me see myself through Your eyes. Faithful. Growing. Becoming.

Amen.

Week Four

Walking in Wholeness

Isaiah 61:3 (NLT) *"To all who mourn… He will give a crown of beauty for ashes, a joyous blessing instead of mourning, festive praise instead of despair."*

Prayer to Begin the Week:

Jesus, I'm ready. I say yes to walking in the new. No more shrinking. No more hiding. Help me rise with boldness, softness, and joy. Let the world see You through my healing.

Amen.

Day 21

DEVOTIONAL

You're Right on Time

Ecclesiastes 3:11 (NIV) *"He has made everything beautiful in its time."*

There were days I looked at my life and whispered, "I should be further by now."

I saw people hitting milestones, building careers, walking in confidence, healing faster—and I felt *so far behind.*

Like I missed something. Like I wasted too much time. Like my pain had delayed my purpose.

But here's the truth:

You are not late. You are not behind. You are right on time—for *God's* time.

He's not rushing you. He's not comparing you. He's not disappointed in how long it's taken you to heal, trust again, or believe again.

God doesn't measure progress in milestones—He measures it in surrender.

You are not missing out. You are *becoming.*

And everything He's promised? It's still ahead. *Right on time.*

Reflection

Where have you felt "behind"—in healing, success, faith, or purpose?

Ask yourself: Who told me I was running late—and what does *God* say about my timing?

_____

_____

_____

_____

_____

Prayer

Jesus, I've spent too long comparing my journey to others. I've let shame and timelines steal my peace. But today, I trust *Your* timing. I am not behind. I am becoming. And I know You're making all things beautiful—including me.

Amen.

Day 22

DEVOTIONAL

God Can Use This

Corinthians 1:3–4 (NIV) *"Praise be to the God... who comforts us in all our troubles, so that we can comfort those in any trouble with the comfort we ourselves receive from God."*

I used to think I had to be fully healed before I could be used. That God was waiting on me to "get it all together" before He could do anything through me.

But the truth is... He was already using the broken pieces.

The way I showed up for a friend with gentle understanding. The way I listened without judgment. The way I prayed differently — not from a place of perfection, but from one of *knowing*.

Every tear I cried became compassion. Every scar became wisdom. Every "me too" became an invitation for someone else to heal.

You don't have to be perfect to be powerful. You just have to be willing.

And sometimes, the most powerful ministry happens in the middle of your own miracle.

Sis—God can use *this*. Even *now*. Especially *now*.

Reflection

Where have you disqualified yourself because you still feel broken?

Ask yourself: How might God be using this very part of your story to comfort or encourage someone else?

Prayer

Lord, thank You for reminding me that I don't have to be "done" to be used. I give You every part of my healing—the messy middle, the silent battles, the not-yet moments. Use it all for Your glory. If my story can help one other person find freedom—then it's already worth it.

Amen.

DEVOTIONAL

He's Restoring More Than You Think

Joel 2:25 (NIV) *"I will repay you for the years the locusts have eaten…"*

For a long time, I thought restoration meant getting back what I lost. But God showed me something deeper: He's not just interested in giving it *back*. He's interested in giving it *new*.

New joy. New strength. New opportunities. New *life*.

He's not piecing together your past—He's creating something brand new from the wreckage.

Every moment the enemy tried to steal—every year that felt wasted, every heartbreak that made you question everything—God saw it. And He's redeeming it.

You may not even realize what's being restored right now: Your confidence. Your voice. Your softness. Your faith.

Sis, He's not done. He's restoring more than you even know how to pray for. He's rebuilding you brick by brick… and this time, it won't fall apart.

Reflection

What's something in your life that feels "too far gone"—like it could never be restored?

Ask yourself: What if God wants to give me something *better* than what I lost?

Prayer

Jesus, You see every place in me that's been emptied out. Every moment I thought was wasted. I trust You to restore what I've lost—not just how it was, but better than I imagined. Surprise me with redemption. Fill the spaces I didn't even know were empty. And help me receive what You're rebuilding with open hands.

Amen.

Day 24

DEVOTIONAL

I'm Starting to Feel Like Me Again

Ephesians 2:10 (NLT) *"For we are God's masterpiece. He has created us anew in Christ Jesus, so we can do the good things He planned for us long ago."*

For a long time, I didn't recognize myself. The girl in the mirror felt like a stranger. The sparkle in my eyes was gone. The lightness, the laughter, the softness… buried beneath years of pain, survival, and shame.

But healing has this quiet way of bringing you *back to life*. Of waking up parts of you that went quiet. Of reminding you who you were before the world wounded you.

And one day, I caught a glimpse of her again.

Not the broken version. Not the guarded one. The *real me*. The daughter. The dreamer. The redeemed woman rising in purpose and joy.

And I thought: "There you are. I missed you."

Sis—maybe that's where you are now. Not at the end, but somewhere in the middle of rediscovery. And I want you to know: *You are not gone.* You are just coming home to yourself again—the version God always saw, always loved, always fought for.

You are a masterpiece in motion.

Reflection

What part of yourself have you felt disconnected from—your joy, your softness, your strength?

Ask yourself: What would it look like to embrace who I'm becoming without needing to be who I once was?

_____

_____

_____

_____

_____

Prayer

Jesus, thank You for not letting me stay lost in the pain. Thank You for gently restoring the parts of me that life tried to bury. I'm starting to feel like me again—and it's beautiful. Help me keep becoming. Keep healing. Keep shining. Because I know who I am... and I know *Whose* I am.

Amen.

Day 25

I Don't Live There Anymore

Isaiah 43:18–19 (NIV) *"Forget the former things; do not dwell on the past. See, I am doing a new thing! Now it springs up; do you not perceive it?"*

Every now and then, a memory shows up like an uninvited guest. A lie I used to believe. A moment I'd rather forget. A version of myself I thought was gone for good.

And for a second... I feel like her again. Like the mess. The mistake. The girl who didn't know her worth.

But then I remember: I don't live there anymore.

That season? Closed. That pain? Healed. That version of me? Loved... but no longer leading the way.

God did a new thing — and I'm living in it now.

You might still hear echoes of the past, but don't let that trick you into thinking you belong there.

You don't. You've outgrown the shame. You've risen from the ashes. You've moved into freedom.

Let the past know: you've changed your address.

Reflection

Is there a part of your past that still tries to pull you back—even though you've already grown beyond it?

Ask yourself: What truth can I speak over myself today to remind the enemy: *I don't live there anymore?*

_____

_____

_____

_____

_____

Prayer

Jesus, thank You for calling me out of who I was and into who I'm becoming. When the past tries to haunt me, remind me that You've already redeemed it. I am not who I was. I am new. I am free. And I live in grace now—not guilt.

Amen.

My Story Still Matters

Revelation 12:11 (NIV) *"They triumphed over him by the blood of the Lamb and by the word of their testimony..."*

There was a time I looked at other people's stories and thought, "Wow... now *that's* powerful." The radical encounters. The big turn-arounds. The dramatic deliverances.

And I'd shrink. Because my story? It felt quiet. Messy. Not tied up with a perfect bow.

But God stopped me in that thought and whispered: "You don't have to bleed publicly to be victorious privately."

Every part of your journey—the hidden healing, the silent battles, the moments you kept showing up—that's holy.

Your story doesn't have to be loud to be *anointed*. It doesn't have to be neat to be *needed*. And it doesn't have to be like anyone else's to carry *power*.

Sis—your story *still matters*. And someone's breakthrough is on the other side of your testimony.

Don't dim it. Don't compare it. Just tell it.

Reflection

Have you ever felt like your story wasn't "big" or "powerful" enough?

Ask yourself: What would shift in me if I truly believed my story could set someone else free?

_____

_____

_____

_____

_____

Prayer

Jesus, thank You for writing my story with such care and purpose. Even the parts I didn't understand—You're using them for good. I release comparison. I embrace the power of my testimony. And I say yes to being a vessel of healing through my own becoming.

Amen.

Day 27

Joy Is Coming Back

Psalm 30:5 (NIV) *"Weeping may stay for the night, but rejoicing comes in the morning."*

There was a time I forgot what joy felt like. Smiling felt like work. Laughter felt foreign. And the thought of being *happy* again? It almost felt… wrong.

How could I laugh when so much hurt still lived in me? How could I celebrate when healing still felt unfinished?

But slowly—*softly*—joy started returning.

Not in fireworks. In flickers. In quiet moments that didn't demand anything from me. A song. A sunrise. A deep breath. A real smile I didn't have to fake.

Joy didn't crash in—it crept in. And that's how I knew it was real.

Sis, if you've been stuck in survival mode If you've settled into sadness like it's home… Let me speak this over you:

Joy is coming back. And when it does—don't run from it. *Receive it.* Even in the middle of your process.

You're allowed to laugh again. You're allowed to live again. Joy is not a betrayal of what you've been through—It's proof that *you made it through*.

Reflection

When was the last time you felt pure joy—no guilt, no pressure, just lightness?

Ask yourself: What's one small joy I can lean into today... and let it remind me that healing is real?

_____

_____

_____

_____

Prayer

God, thank You for joy—even when it comes in flickers. Help me welcome it without fear or guilt. Let laughter rise again. Let light return. I'm ready to feel free. I'm ready to live light. I'm ready to *laugh without apology.*

Amen.

It's Safe to Be Soft Again

Ezekiel 36:26 (NIV) *"I will give you a new heart and put a new spirit in you; I will remove from you your heart of stone and give you a heart of flesh."*

At some point, I stopped being soft. I stopped crying. Stopped hoping. Stopped letting people all the way in.

Because soft felt dangerous. Vulnerable. Unsafe. Weak.

So I toughened up. Built walls. Carried strength like armor and wore independence like survival.

But underneath the hardness was a girl who still longed to be held. To be safe. To be known. To be *soft.*

And slowly… Jesus started breaking through. Not to scold me. But to *heal me.*

He didn't shame my hardness—He understood it. But He never meant for me to live guarded forever.

And sis? Neither does He for you.

It's safe now. You don't have to carry the weight alone. You don't have to perform. You don't have to protect yourself from love.

You are protected by Him. And in His presence — softness isn't weakness. It's worship.

Reflection

Where have you hardened yourself to survive—emotionally, spiritually, or relationally?

Ask yourself: What part of me wants to feel again... but hasn't felt safe enough to?

_____

_____

_____

_____

_____

Prayer

Jesus, You see the parts of me I've shut down to survive. You know why the walls went up. But now, I want to live soft again. Safe in You. Healed in You. Let my heart be tender again—not so the world can break it, but so *You* can fill it.

Amen.

Final Reflection: Day 30—The Full Cirle

DEVOTIONAL

I'm Not Who I Was— and That's the Miracle

Scripture: 2 Corinthians 5:17 (NIV) *"Therefore, if anyone is in Christ, the new creation has come: The old has gone, the new is here!"*

If you only knew where I started… If you only saw the nights I cried myself to sleep… The secrets I buried. The shame I carried. The silence I lived in. The version of me I thought I'd never escape.

But sis—I'm not her anymore.

Not because I figured it out. Not because I fixed myself. But because Jesus met me in the mess and didn't leave me there.

He loved me through it. He pulled me out. He walked me step by step through the fire—and now?

I'm still standing. I'm still healing. I'm still here.

Stronger. Softer. Bolder. *New.*

And that's the miracle.

Not that it never happened... But that it no longer holds me. That I don't answer to my past anymore. That I look in the mirror and actually *see a woman I love.* That my story didn't end in the valley — it was just where the testimony began.

You are living proof that God still heals, still frees, still redeems. So take a breath, sis. Look how far you've come.

You're not who you were. And that's the miracle.

Reflection

Take a moment to celebrate: What have you overcome that you never thought you would? How are you different now—even if healing still continues?

Ask yourself: What will I carry forward—and what am I finally free to leave behind?

Prayer

Jesus, You did it. You met me in my brokenness and never let go. Thank You for not giving up on me. Thank You for healing what I thought was too far gone. I'm not who I was—and I praise You for that. Let my life be a living testimony. Let my story set others free. Let everything in me reflect Your glory. I'm redeemed. I'm ready. I'm Yours.

Amen.

Final Blessing

You did it.

You showed up. You cried. You prayed. You opened your heart to healing—and Heaven noticed.

This may be the end of a 30-day devotional… But it's the beginning of something beautiful.

You are not the same. And you never have to go back.

May you walk forward with boldness. With softness. With strength. With laughter. With joy. With *fire.*

Let your life be a love letter to the One who redeemed it. And when you share your story, may it set someone else free.

You are a miracle. And the world needs your light.

With all my heart,
Rose

Closing Prayer

Jesus,

Thank You for walking with me through every page, every tear, every breakthrough. Thank You for meeting me in my brokenness and never letting go. I lay my past at Your feet. I surrender the weight I was never meant to carry. Fill me now with holy fire, bold joy, and deep-rooted peace. Seal the healing that has begun. Help me walk forward as the redeemed woman You created me to be—soft, strong, seen, and secure in Your love. Let my life reflect Your glory. Let my story set others free. I am Yours. I am whole. I am redeemed.

Amen.

Scriptures to Carry Forward

Truth for the days ahead. Hope for the heart still healing. Let these verses anchor you in the truth of who you are and the God who never let go. When the enemy whispers lies, when your heart feels heavy, when the past tries to pull you back—speak these out loud. Declare them. Stand on them. These are your weapons and your promises.

Isaiah 43:1 (NIV) *"Do not fear, for I have redeemed you; I have summoned you by name; you are mine."*

Joel 2:25 (NIV) *"I will repay you for the years the locusts have eaten..."*

2 Corinthians 5:17 (NIV) *"Therefore, if anyone is in Christ, the new creation has come: The old has gone, the new is here!"*

Psalm 34:18 (NIV) *"The Lord is close to the brokenhearted and saves those who are crushed in spirit."*

John 14:27 (NIV) *"Peace I leave with you; my peace I give you. I do not give to you as the world gives. Do not let your hearts be troubled and do not be afraid."*

Romans 8:1 (NLT) *"So now there is no condemnation for those who belong to Christ Jesus."*

Philippians 1:6 (NIV) *"He who began a good work in you will carry it on to completion until the day of Christ Jesus."*

Revelation 12:11 (NIV) *"They triumphed over him by the blood of the Lamb and by the word of their testimony..."*

Zephaniah 3:17 (NIV) *"The Lord your God is with you… He will take great delight in you… He will rejoice over you with singing."*

You don't need to have all the answers. You just need these truths—and the God who speaks them over you. Cling to His Word, sis. Let it be your sword, your comfort, and your song.

Final Word from Rose

Sis, if you made it to the end of this devotional—I hope you know how proud I am of you. You didn't just read words… *You showed up for your healing.* You invited Jesus into the deep places. You said yes to redemption—and that changes everything. This journey wasn't about perfection. It was about presence. And now? You carry something sacred. You carry a testimony. So don't stop here. Keep walking. Keep healing. Keep letting the Word of God renew your mind and restore your heart. Your story is holy ground now. Walk boldly in it. And always remember: You're not who you were. You're who He says you are. Redeemed. Radiant. Ready.

With all my love,
Rose

Stay Connected

Want more encouragement, updates, and resources on your healing journey?

Visit **rosemetheny.com**

- *Blog posts, book updates, and more from Rose*
- Join the email list for devotionals, freebies, and behind-the-scenes.
- Explore the full *Redeemed* and *Renewed* collection. Let's keep walking in freedom—together.

You can also reach out directly at:
hello@rosemetheny.com